EXPLORING WORLD CULTURES

Egypt

Kate Shoup

Cavendish
Square

New York

To Heidi and Olivier.

Published in 2016 by Cavendish Square Publishing, LLC
243 5th Avenue, Suite 136, New York, NY 10016

CPSIA Compliance Information: Batch #WS15CSQ

All websites were available and accurate when this book was sent to press.

Library of Congress Cataloging-in-Publication Data

Shoup, Kate, 1972-
Egypt / Kate Shoup.
pages cm. — (Exploring world cultures)
Includes bibliographical references and index.
ISBN 978-1-50260-583-2 (hardcover) ISBN 978-1-50260-582-5 (paperback) ISBN 978-1-50260-584-9 (ebook)
1. Egypt—Juvenile literature. I. Title.

DT49.S54 2016
962—dc23

2014050233

Editorial Director: David McNamara
Editor: Kristen Susienka
Copy Editor: Cynthia Roby
Art Director: Jeffrey Talbot
Designer: Joseph Macri
Senior Production Manager: Jennifer Ryder-Talbot
Production Editor: Renni Johnson
Photo Research: J8 Media

The photographs in this book are used by permission and through the courtesy of: Philip Game/Lonely Planet Images/Getty Images, cover; Wael El Sisi/File:Giza Pyramids with camel.jpg/Wikimedia Commons, 4; Peter Hermes Furian/Shutterstock.com, 6; Cris Bouroncle/AFP/Getty Images, 7; Mountainpix/Shutterstock.com, 8; Mondadori Portfolio via Getty Images, 9; KHALED DESOUKI/AFP/Getty Images, 11; Sylvain Grandadam/age fotostock /Getty Images,13; Jason Benz Bennee/Shutterstock.com, 15; Doug Pearson/Jon Arnold Images/Superstock, 17; Universal Images Group/Universal Images Group/Superstock, 18; Anadolu Agency/Getty Images, 20; DEA/G. DAGLI ORTI/De Agostini/Getty Images, 23; DeAgostini/Getty Images, 25; SALAH HABIBI/AFP/Getty Images, 26; File: By Maler der Grabkammer der Nefertari [Public domain], via Wikimedia Commons, 27; Ashok Sinha/Exactostock/Superstock, 29.

Printed in the United States of America

Contents

Egypt is a very old country. It started in 3150 BCE and has many traditions. Many buildings and statues made in ancient Egypt still stand today.

You can still see parts of ancient Egypt today.

Almost all of Egypt is covered in desert. Most Egyptians live along a river called the Nile River. The Nile River is in the Nile Valley and Nile Delta. It provides water to a harsh, dry land. About half of Egyptians live in cities. The other half live in the countryside.

Most people who live in Egypt are native Egyptians. Like many of their neighbors in the Middle East, they speak Arabic. They follow a religion called Islam. Islam is important to many aspects of modern Egyptian culture.

Egypt has a lot of customs and celebrations. Learning about Egypt can be fun.

Geography

Egypt is in a part of the world called the Middle East. It covers a lot of land—390,000 square miles (1 million square kilometers). Some of Egypt is in Africa and some of it is in Asia. The Mediterranean Sea is to the north and the Red Sea is to the east.

A map of Egypt

There are two deserts in Egypt. They are the Sahara Desert and the Libyan Desert. These deserts take up most of the country. Most Egyptian people live near the Nile River.

The Khamaseen

In the spring, a strong wind called the "Khamaseen" blows. This wind often brings sand and dust. Sometimes, it causes the temperature to rise to more than 100 degrees Fahrenheit (37 degrees Celsius).

Egypt is very dry. Less than one inch (2.54 centimeters) of rain falls per year. In the summer, Egypt is very hot. It is cooler during the winter.

FACT!

Egypt has more than 15,000 types of animals. About 10,000 of these are bugs.

Egypt was one of the world's first countries. The kingdom of Egypt started in 3150 BCE. The leader of this kingdom was called the pharaoh. One of the most famous pharaohs is Tutankhamen, who is

A mask of King Tut. He is sometimes called the "Boy King."

also known as "King Tut." He was nine years old when he became the ruler of Egypt.

FACT!

For a long time, no one knew about Tutankhamen. A man named Howard Carter found his tomb in 1922.

The kingdom of Egypt lasted for three thousand years. After that, it was run by outsiders. First, the Persians took over Egypt. Then came the Romans, the Byzantines,

King Fuad I

the Muslim Arabs, and the Ottoman Turks. After that, the French and the British ran Egypt. Finally, in 1922, Egypt became free. Egypt crowned a new king, King Fuad I, that year.

A Republic

In 1952, Egypt became a **republic.** A republic is a country run by people who are elected, instead of by a king or queen.

Government

Egypt's official name is the Arab Republic of Egypt. Its government is made up of three parts:

- Legislative: This part of the government is called "Parliament." People in Parliament write new laws.

- Judicial: This part of the government is made up of the courts. In Egypt, the judicial branch is based in part on Islamic law.

- Executive: The president and prime minister make up this part of the government. The president is the head of the state. The prime minister is in charge of the government.

FACT!

The Egyptian Parliament has at least 450 members. They meet in Cairo, the nation's capital.

Women and Government

Women are allowed to be members of the Egyptian government but very few are. In the last Parliament, only 1.8 percent of the members were women.

Egypt's Constitution describes the country's basic laws. It was written in 1923, but it has been changed several times since then. All Egyptian citizens eighteen years and older can vote in Egypt's elections.

Egypt's Parliament building

The Economy

Egypt is one of the richer countries in the Middle East. Its **economy** is growing.

The Poor in Egypt

Even though Egypt is one of the richer countries in the Middle East, there are many poor people living there. In fact, many Egyptians earn less than $2 per day.

Some Egyptians are farmers. They grow crops along the Nile River. Other Egyptians work in factories to make cars and clothing.

In Egypt, a big part of the economy is tourism. Many people visit Egypt each year to see its historic sites, such as the Sphinx and the Great Pyramid of Giza. They stay in hotels and eat

In 2013, more than 9.5 million people visited Egypt.

in restaurants. This brings a lot of money into the country.

In 1869, a 120-mile (193 km) canal called the Suez Canal was built in Egypt. It opened a trade route from Europe to Asia. The Suez Canal has had a big effect on world trade.

Historic sites such as the Sphinx and the Great Pyramid of Giza attract millions of tourists each year.

The Environment

All people, plants, and animals need clean air and clean water to live. In Egypt, however, much of the air and water is dirty. We see this in big cities, such as Cairo and Alexandria.

One reason the air is dirty is that it does not rain a lot in Egypt. Another is because of smoke from cars and factories. Egypt's poor sewer system and chemicals used on farms pollute the water. Many people and animals suffer because of pollution. Egypt is working to fix these problems.

Pollution by Noise

Noise pollution is a big problem in Egypt. The city of Cairo is very loud. Being there is like being inside in a loud factory!

Air pollution is a big problem in Egyptian cities such as Cairo.

FACT!

For a long time, a group of people called the Zabbaleen has picked up trash in Cairo. They recycle 80 percent of the trash they pick up. American garbage collectors recycle only 30 percent!

The People Today

Egypt has more than 82 million people. It has the most people of all the countries in the Middle East, and is the fifteenth most populated country in the world. While most Egyptians live along the Nile River, some live near the Suez Canal or in desert **oases**.

Most people who live in Egypt come from the same group. They are called ethnic Egyptians. Ethnic Egyptians make up 94 percent of the

How People Live

About half of Egyptians live in cities, such as Cairo, Alexandria, Giza, and Luxor. The other half—called *fellahin*, or farmers—live in the countryside.

Many believe that people who live in Egypt are Arabs, but people who live in Egypt call themselves Egyptians.

country's population. Other groups in Egypt include the Abazas, Turks, and Greeks, as well as tribes such as the Bedouins. These groups are quite small.

About half of Egyptians live in cities.

Lifestyle

About half of Egyptians live in the countryside. These people have a much different lifestyle from those who live in Egypt's big cities.

Egyptians in the countryside live off the land.

Egyptians in the countryside live off the land, much like ancient Egyptians did. In fact, they often work with the very same tools their ancestors used. People who live in the cities enjoy a more modern lifestyle, with cell phones and televisions.

Family Matters

No matter where they live, Egyptians consider family important. Often, several family members live together in one home, especially in the countryside.

In the past, Egyptian women did not have the same rights as Egyptian men. For example, in some courts of law, a woman's **testimony** was worth only half of that of a man. Lately, however, things have changed. In January 2014, Egypt signed a new Constitution that gives women the same rights as men.

FACT!

Many Egyptian women wear a hijab—a scarf that covers their hair.

Religion

Some Egyptians are Christians. Some are Jews. However, most Egyptians—about 90 percent—are Muslims. Muslims are people who practice the religion of Islam. They worship in buildings called mosques.

FACT!

Islam is Egypt's official religion. Islam's laws, called **sharia**, are the root of many of Egypt's own laws. Some of these laws are quite strict.

Many Egyptians worship at mosques like this one.

Worshipping Gods

Early Egyptians worshipped many gods. This is called **polytheism.** Ra was the name of the sun god. Isis was the goddess of life and magic. Early Egyptians also believed that the pharaoh was a descendant of the gods.

Egypt is not known for its religious freedom. In fact, when it comes to religious freedom, Egypt is the fifth worst country in the world. This is partly because Egypt allows only three religions: Islam, Christianity, and Judaism. Egyptians who practice other faiths or no religion at all are often bullied or mistreated.

Language

Modern Standard Arabic (MSA) is the official language of Egypt. It does not use the same letters as English (A, B, C, and so on). Instead, it uses the Arabic alphabet. The letters in this alphabet are written from right to left. Many Egyptians also learn English in school.

FACT!

Most Egyptians speak a different type of Arabic as they go about their daily lives. It is called "Egyptian Arabic."

The ancient Egyptians did not speak Arabic. They spoke Egyptian. In written form, this ancient language used symbols rather than letters. These symbols, called **hieroglyphs**, looked like small drawings.

The Rosetta Stone

By the fourth century, Egyptians no longer used hieroglyphs. In time, people forgot how to read them. In 1799, explorers found the

The Rosetta Stone allowed scholars to read hieroglyphs again.

Rosetta stone. It was a rock on which words had been carved in many languages, including hieroglyphs and Ancient Greek. After that, people learned how to read hieroglyphs again.

For thousands of years, Egyptians have enjoyed the arts. All around Egypt there are beautiful paintings, sculptures, and buildings. Many of them are very old. Egyptian writing also goes back thousands of years.

FACT!

The ancient Egyptians were one of the first people to use scrolls for writing. These scrolls were made from papyrus. To make ink, Egyptians mixed burned wood with water.

Today, the Egyptian people enjoy watching movies and television shows. Egyptian music is also very popular. Egyptians also like going to museums. The Museum of Cairo has many artifacts from ancient Egypt.

The Invention of Music

According to the ancient Egyptians, music was invented by a god named Hathor.

Egyptians have been playing musical instruments for centuries.

Egyptians enjoy several festivals and holidays each year. One is Sham en Nisim. This is an old holiday that marks the start of spring. Egyptians also celebrate Labor Day, Revolution Day, and Armed Forces Day. Religious holidays such as Eid Al-Fitr and Eid Al-Adha are also important.

Fun and Play

Egyptians love soccer (which they call football). Soccer is Egypt's national sport. The Egyptian national team is called the Pharaohs. There are also several soccer clubs all around the country. Two of these, El Ahly SC and Zamalek SC, play each year in a match called the Cairo Derby. For Egyptians, this game is the best part of the soccer season.

FACT!

The Pharaohs have won a big soccer competition called the African Cup of Nations seven times. However, they have qualified for the FIFA World Cup only twice.

A Pharaoh player (in red) blocks an opponent.

Basketball is another popular sport. Egypt's national team, called "Team Egypt," has won sixteen medals at the International Federation of Basketball African Championship.

Ancient Egyptians played a board game called *senet*. It had a game board with thirty squares and two sets of game pieces called "pawns."

The Mystery of Senet

No one knows how senet was played in ancient times. Today's players have developed their own set of rules.

Queen Nefertari playing senet. Her invisible opponent is fate.

Food

Farmers in Egypt grow beans and vegetables. These are very common foods in Egyptian meals. In Egypt, meat is very expensive. For this reason, many Egyptian dishes are vegetarian.

A blend of rice, lentils, and macaroni, called *kushari*, is Egypt's national dish. Mashed fava beans, called *ful medames*, are also popular.

Fasting at Ramadan

During the religious month of Ramadan, Muslims fast—or don't eat—during the day. When they break the fast each evening, many Muslims celebrate with special meals. They eat these meals with their extended families.

In Egypt, almost all meals are served with bread. Egyptians eat a type of flatbread called *eish masri*. For dessert, Egyptians enjoy sweet treats such as *basbousa* and *baklava*.

Egyptians drink a lot of tea. Egyptian tea is dark and sweet. There are two types of Egyptian tea: Koshary and Saiidi. Cafés are popular places to drink tea.

FACT!

The word *eish masri* means "to live" or "to be alive." In Egypt, bread is central to life!

Eish Masri is important bread in the Egyptian diet.

Glossary

economy The process by which goods and services are produced, sold, and bought in a country or region.

hieroglyphs Symbols in Egypt's ancient writing system.

noise pollution A problem caused by a noisy environment.

oases Areas in the desert where water is found.

polytheism A belief in worshipping many gods rather than just one.

republic A country governed by elected people, rather than a king or queen.

sharia Islamic laws; these laws influence many of Egypt's laws.

testimony A statement given in a court of law.

Find Out More

Books

Boyer, Crispin. *Everything Ancient Egypt*. National Geographic Kids. Washington, DC: National Geographic Children's Books, 2012.

Hart, George. *Ancient Egypt*. DK Eyewitness Books. New York: DK Children, 2014.

Websites

History for Kids: Understanding Ancient Egypt

www.historyforkids.net/ancient-egypt.html

TIME for Kids Around the World: Egypt

www.timeforkids.com/destination/egypt

Video

Discovery Channel Egypt Videos

www.discovery.com/life-topics/other/other-topics-egypt-videos.htm

This page offers links to several videos about Egypt.

Index

About the Author

Kate Shoup has written more than twenty-five books and has edited hundreds more. When not working, Kate, an IndyCar racing fanatic, loves to ski, read, and ride her motorcycle. She lives in Indianapolis with her husband, her daughter, and their dog. To learn more about Kate and her work, visit www.kateshoup.com.